D0606811

Howarth, Sarah.
Roman people /
1995.
33305003710880
LA   05/19/95

ROMAN PEOPLE

Sarah Howarth

SANTA CLARA COUNTY LIBRARY

3 3305 00371 0880

The Millbrook Press
Brookfield, Connecticut

For the memory of Fr. T. D. Healy

Published in the United States in 1995 by
The Millbrook Press
2 Old New Milford Road
Brookfield, Connecticut 06804

First published in Great Britain in 1993 by

Simon & Schuster Young Books
Campus 400
Maylands Avenue
Hemel Hempstead
Hertfordshire HP2 7EZ

Designed by Neil Adams
Illustrations by Philip McNeill

Text copyright © 1993 by Sarah Howarth
Illustrations copyright © 1993 by Philip McNeill

Typeset by DP Press Ltd, Sevenoaks, Kent

Printed and bound by Proost International Book Co., Belgium

Library of Congress Cataloging-in-Publication Data
   Howarth, Sarah.
   Roman people / Sarah Howarth : [illustrations by Philip McNeill].
     p. cm. — (People and places)
   Includes bibliographical references and index.
   ISBN 1–56294–650–1
   1. Rome—Social life and customs—Juvenile literature. 2. Social classes—
Rome—Juvenile literature. 3. Occupations—Rome—Juvenile literature. [1.
Rome—Social life and customs.] I. McNeill, Philip, ill. II. Title. III. Series:
Howarth, Sarah. People and places.
DG78. H678 1995
937'. 0099—dc20
                                                      94–33578
                                                          CIP
                                                          AC

Picture acknowledgments

Picture research by Donna Thynne

Front cover: The Bridgeman Art Library
Spine: The Bridgeman Art Library

Ancient Art & Architecture Collection: p. 22; Archiv für Kunst und Geschichte:
pp. 8, 14, 21, 24, 42; British Museum: frontispiece, pp. 6, 7, 10, 35, 43; Michael
Holford Photographs: pp. 11, 15, 18, 23, 31, 40; Magnum Photos/Eric Lessing
Archive: pp. 26, 27; The Mansell Collection Ltd: contents page, pp. 13, 16, 17,
20, 28, 29, 32, 33, 36, 37, 41, 44, 45; Scala: pp. 9, 34, 38, 39; Jason Wood
Photographs: pp. 19, 25.

CONTENTS

INTRODUCTION

Imagine you had to tell someone from another planet about life in the twentieth century. How would you do it? One way to begin would be to look at a great world power whose way of life and system of government is copied in many different countries, and then describe how this affects people's lives.

About 250 years before the birth of Christ (B.C.), the city of Rome began to become just such a world power. Its armies and politicians created an empire that, at its greatest, stretched from Britain to the Sahara Desert in Africa, and from Germany to the Euphrates River in the East. The Roman Empire survived for centuries. In Western Europe, Roman power crumbled only in the fifth century of the Christian era (A.D.). In the East, the Empire survived much longer. Here it was based at Constantinople, the city built by the Emperor Constantine in the fourth century A.D. as a new center of Roman government.

By looking at the life and work of different Roman people, you can see how the power of Rome spread from one land to another, and how it gradually changed. In this book, you will find out about people like soldiers and officials, who worked to increase the power of Rome. You can learn about people like gladiators and mosaic workers, who played a part in the distinctive Roman way of life that was copied throughout the empire. In addition to this, you can discover something about people whose beliefs and actions began to challenge the basis of Roman power and led to change.

THE CITIZEN

H ere a lawyer named Pliny the Younger, sent out to govern a Roman province near the Black Sea, writes to the emperor in Rome with a special request: to allow Pliny's doctor to become a Roman citizen:

I ask you to grant Roman citizenship to a doctor who treated me at a time of life-threatening illness.

An honor and a reward

Pliny's request shows us that being a Roman citizen was a privilege highly valued by his contemporaries. This was because Roman citizens were given special rights, and because there was a range of activities in which only citizens were allowed to take part. Only Roman citizens had the right to vote on a range of political issues and to work as government officials. Only citizens could serve in the most important army units, called the legions. Citizens were allowed to own property. If accused of crime, they could ask to have their case heard by special courts in Rome. The New Testament of the Bible records one very famous example of the Roman citizen's right to appeal to Rome, in the story of St. Paul (*c.* A.D. 10–64). When he was arrested in Jerusalem, St. Paul used his right as a Roman citizen to appeal to the emperor, and he was taken to Rome for this purpose. This happened in the first century A.D.

Citizenship was given as an honor and a reward. A Roman historian called Suetonius (*c.* A.D. 69–140) has something to say about this. He describes how Julius Caesar, a high-ranking army officer who controlled the government in Rome in the first century B.C., *"gave citizenship to all the doctors in Rome to encourage them to live there"*. From about the time of the Emperor

This bronze figure was made in Roman times and shows an official called a lictor going about on business. Roman citizens were expected to play a part in public life and act for the good of the community they lived in.

THE CITIZEN

Claudius in the middle of the first century A.D., it also became the custom for soldiers who were not already citizens to be given citizenship when they finished their service in the army. To mark the occasion, each soldier was given a small bronze plaque called a diploma, and the grant of citizenship was recorded on this diploma. Historians use the evidence of objects like these to learn more about the background of different people who became Roman citizens.

Roman citizens outside Rome

As Roman power spread, first throughout Italy and then into other countries, some of the people conquered by the Romans were given Roman citizenship. But the question of who was to be allowed to have the political rights and the important position of a citizen caused

Roman armies conquered many parts of the world. This photograph shows a stretch of Hadrian's Wall, built in the north of England by Roman soldiers. Roman customs were quickly adopted in most of the lands conquered by Rome, and many people were eager to become Roman citizens.

much argument—and even war. Around 100 B.C., a war known as the "Social War" broke out when the people of Italy outside Rome demanded to be treated as citizens. Rome eventually had to give way and grant what they wanted. You can see from this story that Rome was sometimes reluctant to create new citizens. This gradually changed, and in A.D. 213 the Emperor Caracalla granted Roman citizenship to all men in the empire who were free (that is, those who were not slaves) when they were born. But women were not allowed to become citizens.

This model of a hut was made in the Iron Age, many hundreds of years B.C. The first people of Rome lived in a village of simple huts like this. In time this early settlement was replaced by a city of splendid buildings whose citizens were proud of their home.

Acting rightly as a citizen

Citizenship brought many advantages, but it also brought responsibilities. The citizen was expected to take part in the running of the city in which he lived. For some, this meant holding important government positions and devoting time to official work. *"My time is completely taken up with work,"* Pliny complains. *"I go to court, sign requests, prepare accounts, and write an unending stream of letters."*

It was not only time which citizens were called upon to give. Rich citizens were also expected to spend some of their wealth for the good of the community: building bridges, roads, aqueducts, and sewers, and providing public entertainment. *"The Emperor Augustus encouraged citizens to improve the city,"* reports Suetonius, recording how temples, theaters, and other buildings were erected in Rome.

THE MOTHER

Many Romans believed that the most important aim a woman could have was to marry and have children. You can see this idea in the words of a man who lived in the first century A.D.:

In the early days of Rome, women were proud to look after the home and give their time to their children.

"The best of mothers"

A wealthy Roman lady putting on jewels and cosmetics, helped by her slaves. Roman women were sometimes accused of paying too little attention to bringing up their children, which was supposed to be the most important part of any woman's life.

Having children was seen as a duty by many Romans. It was a duty to the family, because it made sure that the family name and spirit would not die out. It was a duty to the state, because the sons would grow up to become citizens and take part in community life, while the daughters would grow up to have sons of their own. These ideas were extremely important to the Romans.

Mothers who had several sons were treated with great respect, and women whose sons played a leading part in the army, or in government, sometimes had influence over their sons' actions. This gave them a position of some power. The Emperor Tiberius

complained that his mother had too much power! The Emperor Caracalla chose to have his mother portrayed on coins as a mark of honor, while the Emperor Nero was at one time so eager to show respect to his mother that he chose a new password for the army—*"The best of mothers."*

Family life

Family life was thought to be very important. Laws were passed to encourage people to marry and have children. The Emperor Augustus was responsible for some of the most famous of these. One law, the "Lex Julia," stated that unmarried men could not receive legacies (gifts in the wills of people who died), and that married men without children had to pay especially high rates of tax. Later laws gave special privileges to parents of more than three children. These laws were intended to protect family life.

Roman law provides one source of evidence about family life, but there are others, such as art and architecture, which often featured scenes of family life. A great religious monument called the Altar of Peace, built on the orders of the Emperor Augustus, is an important example. The walls of the monument are decorated with a frieze showing the emperor and his family taking part in a religious procession. This scene had a message: that family life helped to bring about peace and prosperity. Augustus, like other emperors, often used art to put across his ideas to as many people

This portrait of a woman was painted in Egypt in the second century A.D. Most artistic work was carried out by men, but sometimes women also worked as artists.

This Roman coin shows the Emperor Nero with his mother, Agrippina. Roman people believed that family life was very important, and that the old people of each household should be treated with great respect.

as possible. Historians call this way of spreading political ideas propaganda—this is a word that comes from Latin, the language spoken by the Romans.

A woman's place

Roman law and customs gave women a fixed place in society. Before she married, a woman was under her father's control, and after she married she had to obey her husband absolutely. Some men beat their wives if they were disobedient even in small matters. This happened to many women. People at this time believed that a woman should treat her husband as if he were her master. St. Augustine, a great Christian thinker born in Africa in A.D. 354, tells a story that describes this. He tells us that his mother, Monica, was patient and uncomplaining even though her husband was bad-tempered and neglected her. Hearing other women grumble about men, Monica would tell them that *"the marriage contract bound them to serve their husbands."* Many people at this time would have agreed with Monica and said that women had nothing to complain about.

Women were expected to look after the home and family. In wealthy households the work was done by slaves. But there was one task that the women who ran the household did themselves: spinning wool to make clothes. Even the Emperor Augustus's granddaughters and the other women in his household who were not slaves had this duty.

THE EMPEROR

The power of the Roman emperors and the great impression that it made on people of the time are described by a historian named Appian, who lived in the second century A.D. This is what he tells us about the Emperor Augustus (ruled A.D. 27–14):

A gold statue of Augustus was placed on a column in the Forum. On it these lines were cut: After many years of violence, he brought peace on land and sea.

A time before emperors

Rome was not always ruled by an emperor. Many experiments were made with different forms of government. In the earliest days Rome was ruled by

A scene from Trajan's Column, showing the emperor making a speech to his troops. The Roman army came to have great political influence; the support of the army helped to bring many emperors to power.

13

kings, and after about 500 B.C. it was ruled as a republic. This meant that, instead of power being given to just one man (like a king), it was shared between important officials (such as the two Consuls) and councils, like the Senate. At first, the Senate was a gathering dominated by the heads of Rome's most powerful households, a group of men called patricians. There were also assemblies of poorer citizens—tradesmen and small farmers known as plebeians. In time the plebeians won the right to play a part in the Senate, too, but once more it was only men who were involved. In the first century B.C., the carefully arranged republican methods of sharing power broke down. Violence flared and military leaders seized power. Julius Caesar (102–44 B.C.) was one of the most famous, and most unpopular, of these men.

The first citizen

Statues and monuments were meant to impress upon people who lived at the time how powerful the emperor was. This picture shows part of a giant statue of the Emperor Constantine.

Appian's story tells us about the first emperor, Augustus, who was Julius Caesar's grandnephew and adopted son. He became the most powerful person in the Roman Empire, taking control of Italy and the lands abroad that the Romans had conquered, and putting down anyone who opposed him. This brought an end to many years of violence and civil war.

Augustus ruled in a new way. He announced that he intended to bring back republican methods of government. This did not happen, but Augustus did share power with the senate. He liked to describe himself simply as *"the first citizen,"* giving the impression that he was no more important than other citizens.

"The right to command the world"

In fact, Augustus, like the emperors who came after him, kept under his own control powers that made him far more important than any government official. For example, the emperor was leader of the army, a position that gave great authority. Contemporaries used the title "imperator" to describe this position. Can you see how the modern word "emperor" developed from this old Latin word? The emperor also kept control of the Roman territories abroad, where there were often rebellions and other troubles. He had a great deal of power in the making of laws and could act as a judge in law cases, with the right to order that people be put to death. These powers were known as "imperium." One contemporary summed up the emperor's powers like this: *"He has the right to command the world."*

Too much power

Some people were critical of the emperor's great powers. Because Rome had been a republic for 400 years, the idea had developed that power came from the Senate and people, who were expected to play a part in government. Kings and dictators were hated and feared because they kept power entirely to themselves. You can see this in the work of the Roman lawyer Cicero (106–43 B.C.). Writing about Julius Caesar, Cicero says, *"He used Roman armies to crush the Roman people, robbing them of freedom."*

Some emperors, like Augustus, did not behave in a way that made them unpopular. But others, like Nero (ruled A.D. 54–68), used their power in a cruel and ruthless way, which led to opposition. According to one Roman, when Nero died in political violence, *"There was great rejoicing. Citizens ran through the street."* Nero was not the only emperor to die a violent death in a struggle for power.

Great arches were erected in many parts of the Roman Empire to celebrate battle victories. A Roman traveling to a city in another part of the empire would have found that the architecture there made him feel quite at home.

THE PRIEST

The important part played by priests and priestesses in religious worship is described vividly by the Roman historian Tacitus:

The temple was to be rebuilt. The area was marked out by a line of flowers. On a certain day, the place was entered by a procession of soldiers carrying branches of olive and laurel. Priestesses followed them. The site was made holy by sacrificing a pig, a sheep, and an ox. This was carried out by the praetor [a government official] *and a priest.*

Worshiping the gods

This statue shows a woman preparing to take part in a religious ceremony. As you can see, Roman artists made their work look very realistic.

The Romans believed in a great number of gods who were thought to control everyday life. In their worship, people hoped to persuade the gods to bring good luck, and stop them bringing bad luck. They did this by praying, asking for their wishes to be granted, and making religious vows (promises), saying that they would make a special gift to the gods if the gods gave what they wanted. Something like this happened in a village in Scotland near the great Antonine Wall built by the Romans in A.D. 142–143, where a special stone was set up to give thanks to the god, Jupiter. On it were carved the words, *"To Jupiter, Greatest and Best. The people of the village at the fort pay their vow willingly."* It was not at all unusual for people to show their religious belief like this.

Acting for the people

Some religious worship—making prayers and vows, for instance—was carried out by the people themselves, without a priest. Priests were involved on great religious occasions when the people felt that someone with special authority was needed to act for them. The description by Tacitus at the beginning of this chapter tells about such an occasion.

There were a number of different groups of priests in Rome. Each had slightly different duties. The most important were the pontifices, who were consulted on many religious matters. Other groups of priests

The Emperor Marcus Aurelius about to make a sacrifice to the gods. Men with political power often had religious duties, and the emperor had special responsibilities. He was the chief priest, the pontifex maximus.

included the augurs, haruspices, and flamines. It was believed that augurs and haruspices were able to tell people about what the gods wanted, and what they intended to do. The flamines were different. Each was devoted to the worship of one particular god or goddess, such as Jupiter, Mars, or Flora.

All these tasks were performed by men acting for the people of Rome. But a very small number of women also had a part to play. These were priestesses dedicated to the worship of the goddess Vesta. Their main duty was to burn a sacred fire, day and night, in the temple of Vesta in Rome.

Religion and power

Few priests devoted all their time to religious duties; most were involved in government and politics, too. The emperor acted as the chief priest, the pontifex maximus, and other officials also acted as priests. These things show us that for the Romans, ideas about religion and ideas about politics were closely linked. When the famous Roman governor Pliny the Younger (c. A.D. 61–113) was made a priest, he wrote a letter to a friend describing his feelings just after this happened: *"Thank you for congratulating me now that I have been appointed an augur. It is a great honor."*

This carving comes from a Roman temple built at Bath, in England. As Roman power spread from one land to another, people with different religious beliefs mixed together and shared their ideas. At Bath, the Romans began to worship a goddess who was already worshiped by the people of that area.

Men as gods

At this time, it was widely believed that someone with great political power and responsibility also had great religious power and responsibility. This idea led to the emperor being treated as if he were a god. An important part of a priest's duty was to see that people joined in religious ceremonies worshiping the emperor. In towns throughout the Roman Empire, special priests were appointed for this task. They punished people who refused to take part in these religious ceremonies, such as the Christians.

THE CENTURION

Centurions were important officers in the Roman army. Here the great Roman leader, Julius Caesar, describes two centurions who served on campaign with him in Gaul (modern-day France) in 54 B.C.:

There were two very brave centurions in the legion. They often argued about which of them was the best soldier, and each year the chance of promotion would make them quarrel.

This figure of a centurion comes from a Roman tombstone. Evidence like this helps us to piece together a picture of the past: Here we can see how centurions dressed. Information about the person who had died was also carved on the tombstone. This figure was carved for the tomb of a centurion named Facilis, who served with the Twentieth Legion in Britain.

Toughness and organization

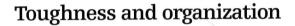

To understand why the centurion was such an important figure in the Roman army, we first need to know something about the army itself.

The Roman army was a very effective fighting force. Few people who saw it in action had any doubt why this was so. Toughness, thorough training, determination—and organization—were the qualities that observers remarked on. A man named Josephus, who watched Roman armies put down a rebellion by the Jews in Galilee in A.D. 66, was just one of the writers who mentions these qualities.

Strict rules set out how the Roman army was organized and how it fought. The army was made up of a number of units called legions. Each legion was commanded by an officer known as a legate, who was appointed by the emperor. The legion was broken down into smaller units. The smallest was the century, which consisted of about 80 men commanded by a centurion. Six centuries joined together to form a larger group called a cohort. There were ten cohorts in each legion.

Soldiers who served in the legions were called legionaries. Only Roman citizens were allowed to fight as legionaries. The Roman army also included troops who were not citizens; they were called auxiliaries.

Leading the troops

It was the centurion's job to train the legionaries as soldiers and lead them in battle. There were many

different skills to be taught. Men who joined the legions had to learn to march so that they could cover almost 20 miles (30 kilometers) in five hours. They were trained to use their weapons—a special spear for throwing, a javelin, and a short sword. They also had to learn how to make camp quickly and according to set rules. The centurions were responsible for making sure that all these exercises were carried out properly. Soldiers whose work did not satisfy the centurions would be punished. Each centurion carried a special stick that he used to beat lazy or disobedient soldiers.

Roman soldiers in action. Those on the right protect themselves by arranging their shields like a wall as they advance. This formation was called a tortoise.

In terror of Rome

A Roman historian who described how large parts of Britain were conquered in the first century A.D. says that Roman armies had won so many great battles that people went in terror of the power of Rome. There is exaggeration in his words—but there is truth as well. Roman armies had conquered many of the countries known to the people of Europe at this time. Many of these lands had been won while Rome was ruled as a republic, so that by about 133 B.C., Rome was the greatest power in the Mediterranean. Under the Roman emperors, there were more battles and more conquests until, towards the end of the first century A.D., a very large area—from Britain and the North Sea to the

Euphrates River in the east to the Sahara Desert in the south—fell under Roman power.

War brought great riches to the Romans. Here the soldiers who attacked and defeated Jerusalem in A.D. 70 carry booty away from the city.

A power in Rome itself

It was not only by conquering foreign lands that the Roman army became respected and feared. Powerful army leaders, backed by their troops, also came to play a great part in the politics of Rome itself. Legates and some of the other most important army officers did not spend all their life as soldiers. They came from high-ranking Roman families involved in politics and they were expected to spend a few years in the army as part of their political careers. Some army leaders became emperors by using their troops to seize power in Rome. The soldiers of Emperor Vespasian (ruled A.D. 69–79) even threatened to kill him unless he agreed to become emperor. Under Augustus, the first emperor, Roman politics had been peaceful. But as the army grew more powerful, civil war and violence broke out again; in the third century A.D., for example, emperors were thrown from power every few years.

THE HOSTAGE

When the famous Roman army leader, Julius Caesar, planned to invade the land of Britain in 55 B.C., the news greatly alarmed the Britons. Caesar's own words tell us what happened next:

Merchants brought this news to the Britons. This led many tribes to send messengers to Caesar. They offered to give hostages and obey Rome.

Signs of good faith

The sort of arrangement Caesar describes was not unusual at this time. For one group of people to give some of its men, women, or children as hostages to another group of people was a sign of good faith. The people giving hostages meant to show that they would keep their word. Hostages were given to guarantee many political promises. Caesar took hostages from some British tribes to try to make sure that they would not rebel against the Romans. In Germany, some tribes, like the Treveri, who lived near the Rhine River, exchanged hostages as a sign that one tribe would pay money to another.

The Roman Emperor Valerian is defeated and bows before his conqueror, King Sapur of Persia.

Political threats

Caesar's story about the Britons suggests that they offered hostages of their own free will. But few hostages were given freely. Usually they were demanded from conquered people by those who

defeated them. The hostages became prisoners, and their lives were in danger if a rebellion in their homeland broke out. In this way, taking hostages was a means for one people to make threats and hold political power over another people.

The friends and enemies of Rome

Rome conquered many different countries. Once fighting was over, however, peaceful relations were set up. The Romans tried to hold on to their power by introducing a Roman way of life rather than by using armed force. This arrangement often worked.

Words cut in stone to record the building of a temple in the south of England tell us a lot about this process. The temple was built soon after the Emperor Claudius established Roman power there in A.D. 43. The man who gave orders for its construction was a Briton, but the inscription (words cut in stone) shows that he was rapidly adopting Roman customs. It says: *"This temple*

This mosaic was made in Africa in about A.D. 500. It shows a Vandal riding away from his house. The Vandals were one of the tribes whose attacks weakened the power of Rome. But as you can see, some parts of the Roman way of life—like living in luxurious country houses—appealed to these tribes.

is dedicated to the gods Neptune and Minerva for the good of the Emperor. Tiberius Claudius Cogidubnus willed this to happen." These words reveal three very important things: Cogidubnus was honoring Roman gods and the Roman emperor; and he had even added the emperor's names (Tiberius Claudius) to his own, a mark of respect showing that he had become a Roman citizen. In ways like these, Roman influence spread throughout different lands.

Prisoners under guard. War brought many captives for the Romans. Some were made to work as slaves.

Areas that did not settle peacefully under Roman rule were treated harshly. A great stone arch called the Arch of Titus, which was erected in the Forum in Rome in A.D. 81, gives us a glimpse of how the enemies of Rome were treated. It shows the triumph (procession by a victorious Roman army) that celebrated Roman victories over the Jews. Prisoners and booty from Jerusalem were paraded through the streets of Rome for all to see. Death or slavery awaited captives like these.

Rome in peril

For many years, Rome defeated its enemies and expanded the area it controlled. But from about the time of the Emperor Hadrian (ruled A.D. 117–138), this began to change. Armies stationed on the frontiers of Roman territory were threatened by the attacks of people like the Goths, who lived north of the Danube River in Germany, and the Persians in Asia. Land was lost to these raiders, and now Roman soldiers sometimes became hostages and prisoners. This happened to the Emperor Valerian in A.D. 260. In the fourth and fifth centuries, pressure increased, and in A.D. 410 the city of Rome itself was devastated by an enemy army.

THE GLADIATOR

The gladiator was a specially trained strong man who fought in fierce competitions. One account of how the people of Rome and other cities liked to watch gladiators fight was written by St. Augustine (A.D. 354–430), a great Christian thinker from Africa:

All my friend Alypius wanted to do was watch the gladiators.

A cruel sport

Because of his Christian beliefs, St. Augustine hated the gladiators' competitions. He called them *"cruel and bloodthirsty."* But for many Romans, a visit to the amphitheater (a stadium built specially for these "games") was an extremely popular pastime. They liked to watch people being killed, with music played to increase the excitement.

Many gladiators were prisoners whom the Romans had taken in battle, or men condemned to death for crime. Some were slaves. Older gladiators trained them to fight using a variety of different weapons. Some gladiators fought as net men, armed with a net and trident (a three-pronged spear). A net man fought against a gladiator armed in a different way, perhaps against a Samnite gladiator with a curved sword and a shield. The net man had to dodge the sword thrusts of his opponent and throw his net to make his opponent trip and fall. The difference in weapons meant that the

Special arenas called amphitheaters were built to stage fights between gladiators and other "games." Look at this picture of the amphitheater at Arles (in modern-day France), with its rows of seats. Were large crowds expected, or small ones?

25

battle was not a match between equal opponents. It was a fight to the death: The winning gladiator killed his opponent.

Men and beasts

Battles between men and wild animals were also very popular with the Romans. These were called venationes—wild beast hunts. One Roman writer describes this sort of display in these words: *"On one day, 20 elephants fought against men armed with spears. Under the Emperor Claudius and the Emperor Nero, men were pitted against elephants, one against one. This was the greatest moment of many gladiators' careers."* Lions, elephants, leopards, tigers, and other animals were specially captured in many parts of the Roman Empire for this purpose. Sometimes the animals were set against each other—a bear against a buffalo, for example. Sometimes armed men hunted and killed great numbers of animals while the audience watched. You can begin to see the scale of violence when you understand that in A.D. 80, to celebrate the opening of the Colosseum, a great new amphitheater in Rome, more than 9,000 animals were killed in one day.

Gladiators in action. Watching fights between gladiators was one of the most popular Roman pastimes. It was part of the Roman way of life that was carried throughout the empire.

Sometimes unarmed men and women were thrown into the arena to be killed by wild beasts. This was occasionally used as a punishment. Some emperors, such as Diocletian (ruled A.D. 284–305), condemned many Christians to death in this way because of their religious beliefs.

Spectacles of this sort cost many men and women their lives. Historians believe that many, many thousands of people were killed as "entertainment."

Racing was another very popular Roman sport. A stadium known as a "circus" was used for races between charioteers with teams of horses, like those shown here.

Differing views

The first contests between gladiators in Rome took place around 250 B.C. As Roman power spread to other countries, they quickly became popular elsewhere and amphitheaters were built in many parts of the empire, from Nîmes and Arles in modern-day France to El Djem in Tunisia. Many people enjoyed watching scenes of bloodshed and brutality. To become popular, politicians encouraged the games and often paid for displays themselves. But gradually some people began to speak out against these horrific shows. A man from Spain named Seneca, who acted as an adviser to the Emperor Nero and who also became famous as a great thinker, was one of those who criticized the games. He said, *"I went to a contest at lunchtime. They are scenes of murder and nothing more."*

An end to the games

Seneca lived in the first century A.D., but it was several hundred years before many people really held views like his. Christians especially opposed the cruel games that took place in the amphitheater. As more people became Christian, and even the emperors took up the new religion, feeling mounted and the contests of gladiators came to an end.

THE TAX COLLECTOR

People in lands throughout the empire paid taxes to Rome—and disliked the men who collected the taxes. A great Roman lawyer named Cicero explains how, in Sicily, the tax collectors had won a particularly bad reputation:

"When Verres was governor of Sicily, the tax collectors ruined the country, taking every man's possessions. Yet only one part went as tax to Rome: the rest went to Verres."

Money for the state

The government needed to raise money to pay for many things. Two expenses were especially high on the list: providing free wheat for the people of Rome, and paying the soldiers of the Roman army. To do this, taxes were demanded from the people. There were many different kinds of taxes. In the centuries before Christ, Roman citizens had to pay a tax called the tributum. This was one of the special responsibilities of being a citizen. Not all taxes were paid in money. Some

Country people coming to pay their taxes to Roman collectors. When the Roman army was winning battles and conquering new lands, riches poured into Rome.

were collected in goods—as supplies of food for the army, for example. Taxes paid in goods became very common during the time of inflation (great price increases) under the Emperor Diocletian in the third century A.D.

Money for the tax collectors

It was not only the government that received the money and goods paid as taxes. Cicero's story shows us that many tax collectors took a share, too. Some officials, like Verres, the governor of Sicily, saw their work as a way of growing wealthy by any means, honest or

Although Rome was a wealthy city, with many magnificent buildings, there were also large numbers of poor people without work who lived there. The government used part of the money it collected in taxes to give free food to the people. Here a group of families are being given help.

dishonest. Many disapproved of this outlook; it did not fit in with the Roman ideal of the good citizen who worked for the benefit of the community without thinking of his own interests.

But although officials like Verres were criticized, many tax collectors were expected to make money for themselves; this was simply part of their arrangement with the government. These tax collectors were called publicani. They came from wealthy families and became tax collectors in order to make more money. From about 200 B.C., groups of these men joined together to buy the right to collect certain taxes for the government. The sum the government was to receive in taxes was agreed, and the tax collectors set to work.

Their aim was to collect far more than the amount they had to pay the government, because anything over this amount they kept as profit. In the days of the Republic, this system of "tax farming" led to very great sums being collected as tax, which caused much resentment. Under the emperors, tax collectors were given fewer opportunities to grow wealthy at the expense of Roman people.

Money from foreign lands

This coin was made in Rome to celebrate the conquest of Britain by the Emperor Claudius in A.D. 43. Coins were often made to mark important events.

As Roman power spread to foreign lands, taxes were demanded from the people who were conquered. This was often very unpopular. In Britain, for example, the high level of taxes was one reason why Queen Boudicca and the Iceni tribe rebelled against the Romans in A.D. 60. Feelings were also strong in other countries, and the writer Josephus (A.D. 37–c. 100), who had acted as the Roman governor of Galilee, tells us that the issue of paying taxes to Rome tempted the Jews to revolt.

In 167 B.C., the government decided that there was no longer any need for Roman citizens living in Italy to pay the important tax called tributum. So much wealth was pouring into Rome as a result of war and conquest that a wealthy future seemed certain.

Depending on conquest

The wealth and goods of foreign lands became more and more important to Rome. Sicily gave grain, Spain had valuable gold mines, and Britain produced silver. Slaves and booty taken in war also brought great riches to Rome. Here a writer of the time describes some of the loot that was paraded in one triumph (victory march): *"A gaming-board was displayed, made of precious stones. One piece was a gold moonstone weighing 30 pounds* [13.5 kilograms]."

Can you think what might happen to Rome if it no longer had these sources of wealth from conquered lands?

THE SURVEYOR

During the second century A.D., a man sat down to make a list of what he thought were the great advantages the Romans had brought to countries they had conquered. Many of these were the sort of projects on which surveyors worked. The Romans, he said,

had measured the world, throwing bridges across rivers, cutting through mountains to make roads and constructing buildings everywhere.

Planning and measuring

Surveyors were involved in many Roman building and engineering projects. Some worked in the army, helping set up military camps and build roads and bridges. Surveyors also worked in towns and cities, where they laid out streets, helped plan the look of the town, and provided a public water supply, drains, and other facilities.

The first task in any of these projects was to send for a surveyor to look at the land and decide what could be done. A letter written in the first century A.D. by the governor of a Roman province in the East tells us about the work of the surveyor. It explains the planning work needed for the building of an aqueduct (special stone channel for water):

"One town here requires a supply of water. I believe water could be brought from a spring about 16 miles [25 kilometres] distant, but there is marshy ground nearby. I have ordered that a survey should be carried out to see if the marshy ground can bear the weight of an aqueduct."

Surveyors worked on many sorts of projects, such as the building of aqueducts. This aqueduct was built in Spain. The engineering knowledge needed for projects like this was spread throughout the empire.

31

THE SURVEYOR

This photograph shows Trajan's Column in the Forum in Rome. It was built to record the Emperor Trajan's victories over the people of Dacia (now part of Romania), and it is 100 feet (30 meters) high. Monuments like this told the people about the power of the empire.

Careful calculations would have to be made to work out the best route for the aqueduct to take, and how it should be built. It was part of the surveyor's everyday work to make such plans, measurements, and calculations.

Bringing water to the towns

To find out more about the projects surveyors helped with, let's look more closely at how aqueducts were built. For the Romans, it was extremely important to provide a supply of water to the towns. This was not just for drinking water, and to flush drains clean, but also to provide water for the bathhouses—and no Roman town was complete without its public baths. Aqueducts were built to meet this demand for water. These aqueducts carried water from its source (a river or lake) to the town in a long channel made of stone. To make sure that the water would flow along the channel, it had to be built at exactly the right angle, and this meant more calculations for the surveyor. He would work out what line the channel should take and give orders to the builders. Sometimes the aqueduct would have to be carried high above ground level on a series of great arches, or it would have to run underground in order to make the water flow easily all the way to town. At the end of the first century B.C., the Roman architect Vitruvius wrote an account of how this was done.

Great engineering and construction skills were needed to build aqueducts. Some covered long distances, like the Pont du Gard, which was built in 19 B.C. to bring water to the city of Nîmes (in modern-day France). It was about 30 miles (50 kilometers) long.

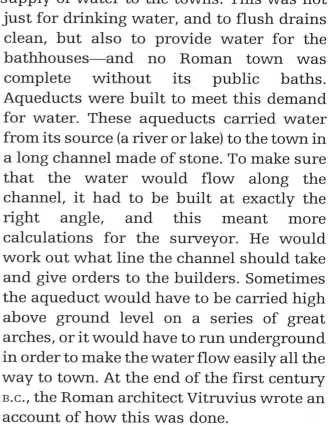

An expensive standard of living

With great building projects like these, the Romans provided a very high level of city services throughout the empire. Some facts and figures show us the impressive scale of their work. In the days of the Emperor Trajan (ruled A.D. 98–117), eight aqueducts served the city of Rome alone. They brought over 235 million gallons (900 million liters) of water gushing into the city each day. Services of this kind were expensive.

From about the middle of the second century A.D., the Roman Empire began to have severe financial problems. Its military power was also threatened at this time. Rome became gradually less wealthy and less powerful until, in the fifth century, it lost control over its lands in Western Europe. Then city life on the Roman scale, with its elaborate buildings and skilled engineering work, faded away. Only in the eastern part of the empire did it survive.

This scene from Trajan's Column shows Roman soldiers building a fort. Surveyors accompanied the soldiers to mark out the lines of the fort.

THE SLAVE

This message was scribbled hurriedly on a writing tablet by a merchant in a Roman city:

Make sure you turn that slave girl into cash.

We do not know who the merchant was, nor the slave girl, but the merchant's words show very clearly what life was like for a Roman slave.

Work, work, work

Slaves were a vital part of the Roman workforce. They were to be found almost everywhere that work was to be done—in the home, in shops and factories, in mines, and in the countryside. Some slaves specialized in particular kinds of work, as barbers, cooks, hairdressers, or candy makers, for instance. The homes of wealthy citizens contained large numbers of slaves who did all the household tasks. The mistress of the household had several women slaves to help her dress, put on her jewels and cosmetics, and look after the youngest children. Educated Greek slaves were often used to teach the older children.

A way to make money

For some people, owning slaves was a means of making money. The Greek writer Plutarch describes how one extremely wealthy Roman named Crassus (*c.* 112–53 B.C.) made money in this way. Crassus kept a group of more than 500 slaves who had been trained as builders and architects. They were

Many slaves were involved in building work. This picture from a Roman tomb tells us something about their hard work. The crane on the left is powered by slaves walking inside the wheel.

used to build houses on land that Crassus bought very cheaply. Then he sold the houses at a high price. These were not the only slaves Crassus owned. Plutarch goes on to list some of the others: *"Crassus owned many excellent slaves—readers, secretaries, silversmiths, waiters."* This list shows us the many different kinds of work undertaken by slaves.

Slaves were also used as the workers on large farms, known as latifundia, in the countryside. The owners of estates like these wanted to make as much profit as they could from their land, and careful calculations were made to work out how many slaves were needed. One man who wrote about farming at this time worked out exactly how many slaves were needed to grow olives in a plot of 160 acres (65 hectares).

Cruelty and kindness

The slave had a fixed position in society. Roman law gave slaves no rights, treating them not as people but as objects. This meant that not only could slaves be bought and sold at the market, but that their masters could treat them as they wished. Slaves could be beaten, or even killed, if their masters chose. Many accounts written by people of the time show us that slaves were indeed often treated very harshly.

But not all slaves were treated badly. Some masters and mistresses were kind to their slaves, and even gave them their freedom. Many freed men and women stayed to work for their old masters. When their masters died, some freed men and women set up tombstones on their graves as a mark of respect. This is a custom that tells us that there

Sometimes slaves were set free by their masters. We know about such events because of the details recorded on tombstones like this one. This stone was put up in memory of two slaves who had been freed.

Female slaves waiting on their mistress. Some slaves carried out very specialized work, acting as teachers, doctors, or architects.

was a strong bond of loyalty between some slaves and masters. Historians use evidence like this to find out about the way slaves were treated. They also use written evidence. These are the words of the Roman philosopher Seneca: *"We Romans are too rude and overbearing to our slaves. They are men as we are: they breathe like us, live like us and die like us."* How did Seneca believe that masters should behave?

Too few workers

Many people who were defeated in battle were taken as slaves by the Romans, so while Roman armies were winning battle after battle, there was always a good supply of slaves. But when Roman territory itself came under attack in the third, fourth, and fifth centuries A.D., this was no longer so. For this, and for other reasons, the Roman government began to find that the empire was short of workers.

THE SHOPKEEPER

Some words scratched on a wall in the Roman town of Pompeii in Italy describe the feelings of all the shopkeepers and traders who lived and worked in this busy town:

Making profit is good.

Setting up shop

In most of the first Roman cities, people used to meet to buy and sell food and different goods in the forum. But as the city developed, this changed. The streets soon became crowded. Some traders set their goods out for sale on the street, while others built shops. Customers came flocking to buy flowers, wine, fruit, vegetables, fish, meat, spices, cakes, medicine, shoes, and the many other wares on display. Sometimes special complexes of shops were built, which were something like modern shopping malls. This happened in Rome, where the

The inside of a Roman shop selling cushions and other cloths. Thanks to the merchants and traders who traveled throughout the empire buying and selling goods, wealthy people had a wide range of choice in the shops.

Emperor Trajan gave instructions for a complex containing 150 shops to be built in about A.D. 100. The ruins of this great market survive today.

Selling goods and making goods

Each shopkeeper sold one main product: the baker sold bread, the cutler sold knives and cutlery, the goldsmith sold articles made of gold, and so on. Some shopkeepers, such as those who sold fruit or vegetables, had to buy their stock. This meant visits from traders who bought food from farmers and then brought it to town

This photograph shows part of the great covered market in Rome, which was created on the orders of the Emperor Trajan. Much Roman building work was on a massive scale: This market contained 150 shops.

to sell to the shopkeepers. Other shopkeepers, like cutlers and cobblers (people who sold shoes), were also craftsmen: They made the goods that they sold. These shopkeepers sat and worked at the front of their shops, hoping that people who came past would be tempted to stop and buy when they saw the goods being made.

The Roman town, its shops full of workers, was a noisy place. Here is a description of the sounds and bustle of a Roman street, written by the philosopher Seneca (4 B.C.–A.D. 65). How many noises does he list? *"There is a great hubbub on every side: carriages rattling in the street, a carpenter working nearby, a man sawing, and a man tuning flutes and horns."*

Shopowners and shopkeepers

Shops were not always owned by the people who ran them. Some were owned by wealthy people as a way of making money. Shopowners like these would use a trusted slave or freedman to look after the shop and run it for them. We know that this happened in the town of Pompeii, for example. Running a shop was not considered a suitable occupation for the most important people in Roman society. You can see that many people held a poor opinion of shopkeepers and craftsmen by reading the words of the lawyer, Cicero, who calls these people *"the lowest of the country."* Feelings like this explain why wealthy citizens used slaves and other workers to run their shops.

The search for riches

One Roman writer said that the Romans set out to conquer foreign lands simply in order to *"search for riches."* This statement was an exaggeration, but it was certainly true that taxes, loot, and goods from conquered lands brought Rome much prosperity, and that much trade took place between the different countries under Roman rule.

However, from about the middle of the second century A.D. the search for riches seemed to have gone badly wrong. The population of the western part of the empire became smaller, the price of goods became higher and higher, taxes rose, and large areas of farming land were abandoned. There were also great military problems that contributed to these economic difficulties. The empire was now under attack, rather than pushing forward for fresh conquests—yet large numbers of troops still had to be paid. The western part of the empire was becoming poor. For shopkeepers and their customers, it was a bad time.

Here two Romans examine the knives and other stock in a cutler's shop.

THE MOSAIC WORKER

As part of a great research project, a Roman named Pliny the Elder (A.D. 23–79) turned his attention to the work of the men who made mosaics. This is what he had to say about one of Italy's first mosaic floors:

The mosaic floor for the Temple of Fortune ordered by Sulla was made from very small cubes of stone. After this time, mosaics were used for vaulted ceilings and were sometimes made of glass.

Everyday scenes and elaborate pictures

As Pliny told us, the first mosaics were made for floors. But soon mosaic workers were also asked to decorate walls and ceilings. Their skill was highly thought of by people at the time. One writer tells a story about the

This picture of a seahorse was created by mosaic workers to decorate a house at Fishbourne in England. Mosaics were very popular with wealthy people throughout the empire.

great soldier Julius Caesar, which shows how valuable mosaics were to their owners. *"Caesar even took mosaic panels with him when he went to fight,"* the account reports.

Mosaic workers, like other craftsmen, were trained when they were young men by older, more experienced workers. The most skilled mosaic workers produced elaborate pictures showing people from legend and history, scenes from everyday life such as charioteers or country people, and pictures of fish, animals, fruit, and flowers.

Patterns in stone

The first mosaics were made by the Greeks, about 400 B.C. They used pebbles, which they set in patterns to make attractive floors for the homes of wealthy and important people. Later, the mosaic worker used sticks of stone, cutting these into little cubes of a regular size called tesserae and setting them into a base of mortar to form his design. Contact with the Greeks led Roman craftsmen to try this skill. Mosaics in different colors were produced by using tesserae of different colored stones. Local stone was used for this. In Italy, mosaic workers used tesserae of colored marble. In Britain, they used chalk for white, sandstone for yellow, limestone for brown and gray, and Purbeck marble for a range of reds, blues, and greens.

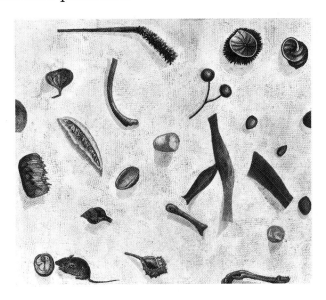

Mosaics showed many different kinds of pictures. This one depicts an odd assortment of things that look like scraps left over from a meal. Historians think that this kind of pattern was linked to the Romans' belief in spirits: The scraps of food were meant to provide food for the household ghosts.

Patterns in glass

Pliny's description also points out another change in the mosaic worker's techniques. This was the use of fragments of glass instead of tiny cubes of stone. Mosaics made from pieces of glass caught the light, glittering and shining. This type of mosaic remained popular for many hundreds of years, right up until the sixth and seventh centuries A.D. At this time, glass mosaics were used for the walls and domed ceilings of important Christian churches. This happened especially in the eastern part of the Roman Empire, lands which became known as the Byzantine Empire.

Mosaic workers trained in the traditions of the Byzantine Empire were responsible for a series of famous glass mosaics in the church of San Vitale in Ravenna (Italy). This church and its mosaics were created in the sixth century on the instructions of the Emperor Justinian.

A mosaic showing actors preparing to give a performance. Highly skilled workers were needed to produce mosaics as complex as this.

From land to land

Just as the fashion for mosaics spread from Greece to Rome, it also spread from Rome to the different lands of the Roman Empire. Villas (country houses owned by wealthy people) were decorated with mosaics in many provinces, from North Africa to Britain and from Sicily to Syria. Having a mosaic floor was a sign that the villa owner was wealthy, important, and eager to live a Roman style of life.

The fashion for mosaics was not the only thing that the Romans took from the Greeks and then spread to the lands they conquered. The Romans had learned many things from the Greeks, and from the peoples of eastern civilizations like Egypt. Now, as the work of Roman artists, architects, thinkers, and writers created interest and enthusiasm in the provinces, the Romans passed on the ideas and skills they had acquired to the people of Western Europe.

The Christian

T he persecution (bad treatment) that was sometimes given to Christians because of their beliefs is described in a letter written by St. Paul, one of the greatest leaders of the early Church:

Three times I have been beaten with sticks; once I was stoned. I have been in danger from my own people, in danger from pagans, in danger in towns and in the country.

A new age

The Christian religion was born in the land of Palestine at the time of the Romans. It spread rapidly, as teachers like St. Paul traveled to many parts of the Roman Empire to tell people the Gospel—the "Good News"—about Christianity.

Christianity was very different from the pagan religions of the Roman Empire. Christians believed that there was only one God, and that Jesus Christ, whom Roman officials in Jerusalem had crucified, was the Son of God. They believed in eternal life after death, and that it was important to lead a good life in the present world.

These beliefs made Christians seem strikingly different to the early Romans. Christians themselves felt different. They believed that history was entering a new age. Before this time, years had been counted from the traditional date of the founding of the city of Rome. Now a new system was started, counting from the birth of Christ. This system is used in much of the world today.

A Roman marriage ceremony, showing man and wife clasping hands. The Christian religion brought new ideas about the importance of marriage and how people should live.

A threat to Rome

For the emperor, and for government officials, it was very important to keep the different lands under their control as a united group. They saw religion as a way to do this. They were prepared to tolerate many different religious beliefs on condition that people gave complete loyalty to the state, and showed this by taking part in public religious ceremonies at which the emperor was worshiped as a god. Christians refused to do this. For this reason they were seen as a threat to the power of Rome.

A struggle to survive

In its early years, the Christian Church had to struggle for its life. Many people were violently opposed to the new religion, and from the time of the Emperor Nero, Christians suffered persecution for their beliefs. Many Christians were tortured and killed. It is believed that St. Paul himself died in this way.

A great change took place when the Roman emperors gave up the worship of pagan gods and came to believe

This picture was drawn in the Middle Ages, and it shows the Emperor Constantine (center) with the Bishop of Rome (left). In a statement called the Edict of Milan in A.D. 313, Constantine declared that it was legal for Christian worship to be conducted throughout the empire.

in Christianity. The most important step was taken when the Emperor Constantine (A.D. 306–337) became a Christian. Christianity no longer had to struggle to survive. It became the official religion of the empire.

A new Rome

At this time, the power of the emperor in Rome was growing weaker. Attacks by Germanic tribes like the Goths and Vandals caused upheaval, until the last Roman emperor was thrown from power in A.D. 476. As Roman government slowly disintegrated, people looked for advice and protection to the leaders of the Christian Church. Bishops and archbishops—and particularly the pope (the bishop of Rome, who was the head of the Church)—began to play an important part in the lands of the old Roman Empire in the West.

But the story of Roman power was not over. At the end of the third century, the Emperor Diocletian had divided the empire into two parts: East and West. The empire in the West, which was centered on the city of Rome, fell apart, while the empire in the East remained strong. In A.D. 326 Constantine decided to build a new capital city there. Built at Byzantium, the city came to be called Constantinople. As people pointed out, it was a "new Rome," a city dedicated to the new religion, Christianity. Here Roman power, changed by Christianity and the Eastern way of life, survived.

Mourners at a Roman funeral. The idea of life after death was not a part of Roman religion, but Christianity promised that believers would live after death. More and more people were won over by the new religion.

GLOSSARY

Amphitheater A stadium built to stage "games," such as fights between gladiators, and wild beast fights.

Aqueduct A water course made of stone to bring water to towns and cities. Sometimes aqueducts ran high above ground level on a series of great arches; sometimes they ran underground. The word aqueduct comes from the Latin language.

Auxiliary A member of the Roman army who was not a Roman citizen. Many auxiliaries came from lands conquered by the Romans.

Byzantine Empire The lands of the Roman Empire in the east of Europe. The Emperor Constantine built a new capital city in these lands, at Byzantium, in A.D. 326. (His new city came to be known as Constantinople.) When Roman power was overthrown in Western Europe, the empire based at Constantinople survived.

Centurion An officer in the Roman army.

Century A unit of the Roman army, consisting of about 80 men.

Citizen A city dweller with special rights and responsibilities. Citizens were expected to play a part in the way the city was run.

Cohort A unit of the Roman army. There were 10 cohorts in each legion.

Empire Lands conquered and ruled by another city or country.

Forum A public square at the heart of many Roman cities.

Games There were three types of pastimes that the Romans described as games. These were the races that took place in the circus, the plays that took place in the theater, and the fights that were staged in the amphitheater.

Gladiator A fighter specially trained to take part in battles that were staged to entertain the public.

Legate The officer who commanded a legion, one of the most important units in the Roman army.

Legion One of the most important units in the Roman army. Its soldiers were called legionaries.

Mosaic A picture made out of small cubes of stone or glass.

Patrician The name given to members of Rome's most important families.

Persecution Harassment and bad treatment. Under many of the emperors, Christians were persecuted because of their religious beliefs.

Philosopher Someone who studies the way people think, and works out ideas about the world.

Plebeian The name given to some of Rome's poorer citizens, such as small farmers and tradesmen.

Republic A way of organizing and governing a country. Rome was ruled as a republic before it was ruled by emperors; at this time the Senate and people were expected to play an important part in politics.

Senate The council in Rome that took an important part in making political decisions.

Slave A man, woman, or child who was not free, and belonged to a master or mistress. Slaves had to work for the person to whom they belonged.

Triumph Procession by soldiers who had won a great victory.

Writing tablet A cake of wax used for writing on. A metal tool called a stylus was used to write on the wax.

FURTHER READING

Artman, John, *Ancient Rome*, Good Apple, 1991.

Corbishley, Mike, *What Do We Know About the Romans?*, Simon & Schuster, 1991.

Guittard, Charles, *The Romans: Life in the Empire*, Millbrook Press, 1992.

Odijk, Pamela, *The Romans*, Silver Burdett & Ginn, 1989.

INDEX